The Soul of a Winner:
5 True Stories of Success

Versandra Kennebrew

Tammy L. Turner

Javay Johnson

Hugh Lee Johnson

Chris Lee

Copyright Information:

Book Cover Design: NT Design Solutions

Editor: Shonell Bacon

Typeset/Formatting/Copy Edit: Claude La Vertu

Publisher: Impact Writers, LLC

The Soul of a Winner:
5 True Stories of Success

Kennebrew/Turner/Johnson/Johnson/Lee

Copyright © 2013 All rights reserved

No part of this book may be reproduced or transmitted in any form or by any means electronic or mechanical, including photocopying, facsimile, recording, or by any information storage and retrieval system, without written permission from the author and/or publisher.

For additional information or to contact for booking information, please visit:

www.TheSoulOfAWinner.com

ISBN: 978-0-615-90112-1

5 True Stories of Success

Table of Contents

Dedication……………………………………….……**5**

Foreword………………………………….…..……..**7**

Introduction……………………………....…….**9**

Chapter 1 – A Message of Love……………...**11**

Chapter 2 – How Poverty Made Me Rich……**23**

Chapter 3 – Potholes to Smooth Roads………**43**

Chapter 4 – From Bus Stop to Won't Stop…...**61**

Chapter 5 – A Leap of Faith: Finding the……**82**
  Courage to Follow Your Dreams

About the Authors……………………………….**96**

The Soul of a Winner

5 True Stories of Success

This book is dedicated to the men and women who have the courage to work through life's struggles and achieve their wildest dreams.

Foreword

I was born a ward of the state, a special needs child who didn't speak for three years. Fortunately for me, an angel - in the form of a woman - adopted me. She touched my soul, spoke to my heart, and brought me to life.

We all need an angel. Sometimes, we need more than one…

Fast-forward to adulthood: I went from receptionist to registered sales assistant at a brokerage house. Now I am Senior Director of Investments for Oppenheimer & Company, and I am a highly sought-after national speaker. That was not by accident; I had to have a plan.

It's been a life of purpose. Not a life limited to financial success, but a life that has been full and meaningful, and most importantly, intentional.

The most important thing you can do in life is to live with intention with a plan, a way to get you where you want to go. And that is the value of *The Soul of a Winner*. It is for anyone who has a dream for a better life. Success is a planned event.

This book will help you make that plan and simplify your journey.

Read *The Soul of a Winner* not just for the inspirational stories; which are great, but also for the "Success-isms" – strategies and tips at the end of each chapter. Adapt them to your personality, your way of doing things. Read them again and again and let them resonate inside of you. Remember them as you live. Highlight what speaks to you and go back to them when you need encouragement or direction. Who knows? One of the tips just may be your breakthrough!

The lessons you will read here, like all life lessons, were learned in the trenches of a life well-lived, a life full of challenges and victories. Most importantly, they are conveyed to you with love from authors who want you to be successful in every conceivable way – from life to love to business.

The Soul of a Winner teaches you how to turn your story into your glory and become an ambassador of change wherever you find yourself, from the home to the neighborhood to the workplace to the world.

Are you ready for your transformation? Are you ready to make a real difference, both in your life and in the lives of those within your sphere of influence? Then this book is for you. Read it, share it, live it...no excuses. And be blessed!

~*Gail Perry Mason*
  Author, Financial Coach

Introduction

Is winning in life really possible for the ordinary person? If so, is success possible for you? My answer is a resounding - yes! But don't take my word for it. Within this powerful book are the true stories of five people, myself included, who despite great hardship achieved their dreams.

What's in another person's story? Wrapped inside every story are the seeds to your success. There is great power in stories. There is even greater power when the story is of a person similar to you. Stories teach, transform, and transmit an energy that you can use to lift you up out of any struggle that you are experiencing.

Why This Book Was Written

This book was born from the desire to bring real change in the lives of those who want more out of life. *"The Soul of a Winner"* was an idea that evolved over the years. Knowing that readers would gain more from a collection of stories than just mine, I approached speaker and author, Javay Johnson with the book idea. My goal was to find others who had a transformational story to share. What happened then was a miracle – beyond anything that I had ever dreamed.

Through Javay, I met speaker/author, Tammy L. Turner, and empowerment coach, Versandra

Kennebrew. Tammy in turn connected me with life coach/author, Chris Lee. By sharing an idea, I was now in the company of four powerful thought leaders who were already on a mission to change the lives of others.

I'm truly honored to present to you this collection of true stories written by the aforementioned authors. Each author's goal was to share with you possibilities available to you to win in life. Success is a learnable skill. Use *"The Soul of a Winner"* as your guidebook to winning on your own terms.

Why You Should Read This Book

This book is for you if you are ready for change in your life. Each author shares their personal story of overcoming seemingly insurmountable hurdles in life. At the end of each story, the author shares three take-aways that we call "Success-isms".

I have to admit that each author's amazing story touched me emotionally, and you will be touched, too. Within every story and each Success-ism, you will learn what is necessary for you, no matter where you are today, to get where you want to go.

You have this book in your possession for a purpose. And that is because you are ready for a real transformation in your life. Turn the page, and let's get started. In the inspiring words of Tammy L. Turner: "Let's Go!"

~Hugh Lee Johnson
Author/Entrepreneur

5 True Stories of Success

Chapter 1

A Message of Love
By Versandra Kennebrew

The Soul of a Winner

A Message of Love

Relax, and incline your ears to this message of love. You are a walking miracle and miracles abound, waiting to be revealed as you call upon them silently when the illusion of lack appears.

You were created by the Creator of all things to create through the power of divine love. In your imagination, thoughts and visions appear to produce miracles for all your brothers to experience. You Are Divine.

For too long you have been in darkness, trapped by the matrix of third dimensional beliefs of separation and limitation. Wake up, my sister. Wake up, my brother. Look to the light and see all that awaits you. Enjoy the abundance that is your birthright. Cast your cares into the river that flows, continuously recycling pain and suffering into joy and peace.

Press the reset button on your limiting beliefs. Delete the terror and despair programming being transmitted through the airwaves. Hit play now, on the program installed on your DNA hard drive in the beginning when God said, "Let there be Light!"

Love and light are all that exists. Give thanks daily for the Son and the Spirit which have guided you through darkness and to the divine light of love.

Prosperity is all around you. Close your eyes and feel it shower you like a foaming waterfall. Feel the mist on your face, covering your eyes, giving you new insight.

Abundant love radiates from your heart, shining brightly with rays that reach out to all man-kind. And so it is.
~ From "Prosperity 2.0.1.3." by Versandra Kennebrew

What do you see when you look in the mirror? Do your eyes immediately zoom in on perceived flaws or imperfections? Has society programmed you to believe you are too fat, too skinny, too nice, too cute, too sexy, too smart, too loud or too quiet? Do you even know who you are underneath the mask you have created with your mind?

Well, ten years ago, my mind was held captive, and the self-imposed chains that I had created choked me until I gave up on life and wanted to die. Suicide was too easy an escape, so the recipe for my slow death was a sprinkle of hopelessness, which led to homelessness. I was tired of the struggles of life.

Three marriages, two miscarriages, a business failure, and Premenstrual Dysphoric Disorder had worn me out. I was trapped in the matrix of third dimensional beliefs of separation and limitation.
-"*Somebody wake me up!*" That was a sweat-dripping nightmare. Sleepless nights, poor emotional and physical health and negative self-talk fueled every fear-based action. The tunnel appeared to get darker and darker. I was an entrepreneur whose spirit had been broken and workman's compensation didn't cover that. Thank God for the shelter. Thank God for my friends who encouraged me and were inspired by my tenacity.

After finding a safe place of refuge, I took a long look in the mirror and discovered my true self. *Jewel* was always there, but her brilliance was distorted by the gridlines of the matrix. Misspoken words and disserving thoughts had manifested a scared and confused woman who felt alone and in despair.

Like in an Intensive Care Unit, a team of experts were divinely assembled. Through loving intention, layers of childhood trauma were peeled back. Societal programming and fear of failure were all dispelled. I was being healed.

A holistic lifestyle and practicing self-care regimens helped me release stress and become more balanced, mind, body and spirit. I began counting my blessings daily. I heard my grandma tell me, "*You are going to make it.*" My soul was set free.

The stronger I became, the more brightly my light shined. No matter what my situation looked like to others, I was being healed from the illusion that I was separated from the source of all things. I was remembering that my creativity was my greatest wealth asset. The old was passing away and a new me was emerging. Deep inside me was the soul of a winner.

Today, I travel around the continent sharing my story of transformation and healing. Much of what I had learned in my life had to be discarded. Like the automotive industry in Detroit recently needed retooling; so did I. My soul needed to be revived. Again, I thank God for the shelter.

Finding a place of refuge was not the end of my dilemma because when a person becomes homeless, they generally have outstanding debt, overdrawn back accounts, poor credit ratings, and are emotionally bankrupt. My local credit union was a great resource that helped me map out a credit repair strategy. My new position as a massage therapy instructor included full benefits and tuition reimbursement. A professional teeth cleaning was finally moving up on the to-do list.

The more trash I discarded, the lighter I felt. I could feel my spirit wanting to soar; as love filled the space where fear once dominated? Daily, I affirmed my worth, my wealth, and my health. I spoke and wrote about the reality I desired. Attaining great wealth and giving back became my new primary thoughts. A renewed attitude of gratitude radiated from me, and everyone could see my light shining brightly. My journal became my memoir, and the more people I inspired and encouraged, the more vivid my visions of success became.

Within five years of starting over again, I paid cash for my first real estate property, was gifted two cars, self-published my first book, received awards from my city government, was featured in multiple print, radio and television outlets, and I was traveling the country, touching the world, empowering women to thrive and not just survive. My spirit was free, and I would never be hopeless again.

Five years later, I was lending my talents as a marketing and community relations specialist to an international retailer. I was teaching my community how to *"eat to live"* and how to become *touch artists*; creating their own touch masterpieces with their hands. I was traveling internationally, teaching entrepreneurs how to ignite their imagination and reinvent themselves. I was serving on the board of directors for one of the state's largest housing non-profits; the Coalition on Temporary Shelter.

So how did I break free from the chains that hold so many back from their purpose and passion? How did I manage to recover after losing my mind to suicidal thoughts and hopelessness? How did I pay back the debts that caused me to be evicted from my home? How did I reinvent myself and become an international speaker and coach?

There is a Buddhist Proverb; "When the student is ready, the teacher will appear." In the world that we live in today, the most amazing teachers are available at our fingertips, 24/7 on the Internet. I did not know any women personally who could mentor me when my life was under construction, so I watched Oprah's show almost daily. Oprah Winfrey was the life teacher I needed to give me a new perspective about wealth. Everything happens in divine order.

One day on Oprah, Mark Victor Hansen and Robert Allen demonstrated to the world how they could generate $1,000,000 in one minute. They were successful. I watched them send an email, and in 60-seconds, more than a million dollars funneled into their bank account.

They then gave the million dollars to Oprah's charity. I wanted to know more about how they did it, so I purchased and read the book *"The One Minute Millionaire: The Enlightened Way to Wealth"*, over and over again. I did not earn a million dollars, but what I took away from that experience expanded my mind so I could achieve wealth beyond my dreams and even purchase the condo I dreamed of when I didn't have a home.

This life-changing event introduced me to the world of Internet marketing, self-publishing, and public speaking as a path to massive wealth. I jumped in with both feet, learning the mechanics of an ever-changing system for wealth. I even learned about real estate, which was an excellent investment that could pay dividends over and over again.

In an effort to seek out local mentors who used similar systems to attain wealth and enlightenment, I began attending seminars and building a network of like-minded individuals with whom I could mastermind with. "No man is an island." I needed a team!

On my journey to becoming an enlightened millionaire, I had to create multiple streams of income and a platform that would allow me to serve while earning. I had to enhance my value, gain new skills and monetize me. To that end, I went back to school to become a self-improvement teacher. I added to my virtual mentor team Internet marketing guru, Stephen Pierce.

I was "on and popping" but with a huge digital divide and perceived economic challenges in Detroit, finding people to value my on-line work was somewhat difficult. One of my friends, Kania Kennedy (who lived in Chicago at the time) and I discussed this mutual challenge, and we inspired one another to add technology and social media coaching to our programming. This was yet another revenue stream.

My expansive social networks became my most valued tool. When it became difficult to make money in my own hometown, I reached out to my supporters across the U.S. and Canada. My most exciting presentation yet has been presenting to a group of holistic health professionals in Montreal, Canada, a workshop on choosing the right coach. I was a little nervous about presenting before a group of French speaking healers, but they made me feel right at home.

Whenever I had the opportunity, I took on paid internships to fine-tune my skills and learn new ones. I was a free agent and could never be an employee again because I had transcended the employee mentality and my creativity could not be turned off. I was no longer a robot: I was created to create.

One of the toughest things I've had to overcome as an entrepreneur has been thinking that the road would get easier. After looking at the characteristics of a journey, ease became irrelevant and the creative experience became most significant. I am a success because of love, and when love is my primary thought, my journey is incredible.

Through my journeys, I have learned that when seeking success, you don't look for money, because cash is not the only currency. As you instead seek out ways to add value to the lives of others, abundance showers you in ways you never thought possible. Miracles are all around us.

I learned from my custom jewelry designer, Benjamin Baker III (of Matrix Atelier) that diamonds do not lose value because they are dirty or have been covered with sediment. Diamonds are the ultimate portable wealth, and a trained eye can spot a diamond in the rough, remove the sediment, and polish it to perfection. You are a diamond no matter what program you are allowing to direct your life right now.

Your success, your wealth, your value is equivalent to your dominant thoughts, words, and deeds. You were created by the Creator of all things to create through the power of divine love. In your imagination, thoughts and visions appear to produce miracles for all your brothers to experience. Incline your ears to this message of love.

Success-isms:

The success-isms and quotes that I share here have stood the test of time, not only in my life but for thousands of personal development and thought leaders. I share these gems with my coaching clients, workshop participants, and mentees around the world. As you expand your perspective and release fear of the unknown, I pray you will experience success beyond your wildest dreams.

* Ignite your imagination

* Be a life-long learner/teacher

* Write, speak and visualize the reality you desire

"All the breaks you need in life wait within your imagination. Imagination is the workshop of your mind, capable of turning mind energy into accomplishment and wealth." ~Napoleon Hill

"Imagination is everything. It is the preview of life's coming attractions." ~Albert Einstein

"An investment in knowledge pays the best interest." ~Benjamin Franklin

"It's easy to carry the past as a burden instead of a school. It's easy to let it overwhelm you instead of educate you." ~Jim Rohn

"Whatever the mind of man can conceive, it can achieve." ~W. Clement Stone

"As you imagine and visualize and verbalize your new story, in time you will believe the new story, and when that happens, the evidence will flow swiftly into your experience. A belief is only a thought you continue to think; and when your beliefs match your desires, then your desires must become your reality." ~Abraham Hicks

5 True Stories of Success

Chapter 2

How Poverty Made Me Rich
By Tammy L. Turner

How Poverty Made Me Rich

I was born and raised in Detroit, Michigan – the "D" as we native Detroiters affectionately call it. I grew up in one of the most desolate neighborhoods in the D, and I went to my neighborhood school; Foster Elementary, which was literally right across the street from the Brewster projects (Brewster-Douglass Housing Projects). My mom and dad divorced when I was two years old. For as long as I could remember, my mom was the sole provider for my brother and me, as I only remember seeing my father occasionally throughout my childhood.

Although I didn't know we were poor back then, I think back to how I would walk to school with a hole worn in the bottom of my shoe because my mom couldn't afford to buy me a new pair of shoes. I remember the cement being cold as we walked to school. But this is where my creativity and determination began to be developed. I found a piece of cardboard at school, and I cut it out in the shape of my shoe, then I inserted the cardboard in my shoe to keep my foot from touching the cement. So, now I'm thinking I'm good and the problem had been solved. That is, until I got on a swing on the playground and the other kids that were standing below me saw the hole in the bottom of my shoe.

It's difficult for a child to understand their youthful role and focus on achieving good grades in class when the other kids are laughing at them and teasing them because of the hole worn in the bottom of their shoe that's slightly camouflaged with cardboard. While the other children were carefree, playing and swinging on the playground, I was already thinking about survival.

As if puberty isn't difficult enough; when you add poverty to the equation, the result is oftentimes disastrous. As I mentioned previously, I didn't know I was poor. I thought my circumstances were normal until I was around other children whose parents would have been considered middle-class. The ongoing theme in our house was "*robbing Peter to pay Paul*". All of my cousins (my mom's sister's children) who lived close by were in similar situations in their homes, so, again, the level of poverty that I experienced, I considered to be normal because I hadn't been exposed to anything else, yet.

We were on welfare or ADC (Aid to Families with Dependent Children) as it was called when I was growing up, which meant that my mom received food stamps and free medical care for us. My brother and I were as happy as kids in a candy store on the day my mom would get her food stamps, because that meant that we could go grocery shopping. Grocery shopping was an event of colossal proportion for us as a family. My mom, my brother, and I would walk to the grocery store, because we didn't own a car, and I must say with each and every step, I was filled with more and more excitement. Perhaps my toes even tingled a bit. It was like walking downstairs on Christmas day. This really was like our mini-Christmas once a month.

My brother and I would skip and sing alongside our mom as if we were going to see the Wizard. When we arrived at the store, I would immediately grab a shopping cart (I always had to be the one to push the shopping cart; I guess I wanted to make sure I had control over those groceries), and my mom would go up and down each and every aisle of the store filling up our basket. She apparently had a system for grocery shopping. She would buy all of her meats, and staples like rice, canned goods, sugar, frozen foods, fruits and veggies, and if there were anything left over, she would allow my brother and I to buy sweets, like Twinkies and Zingers. Oh, how I loved those Zingers.

Because we didn't own a car, my mom would hire a "jitney" (person who sits outside the grocery store with a car to drive people home with their groceries, for cash). The jitney would take us and our groceries home. We would drag everything in to our one-bedroom apartment and then we would unpack the groceries and anticipate dinner that night. This whole process was quite the experience for us, and we would look forward to it once a month. At the beginning of the month when we first received the food stamps, our meals consisted of spaghetti, lamb chops, shrimp, or meatloaf. Towards the end of the month, those meals consisted of fried chicken, corn, or sometimes sardines or canned salmon, because she could add bread and stretch this as a meal.

During my middle school years, I realized that our situation was bleak. When I was twelve, our seventh-grade class had Secret Santa. We were given a limit of $2 to spend on the gifts. I had heard that the person whose name I pulled; Tyrone McAdoo, wanted Run DMC's "King of Rock" song on 45. My gift was a little more than $2, so I asked my mom for the money to get this record, and she told me that we couldn't afford it.

On the day that we were to exchange gifts with the other students, I was reduced to giving Tyrone $2 because the record cost more than what I could afford, and I had no way of getting to a record shop to purchase the song, even if I had the money because we didn't own a car. I was the only child in seventh 7th grade that did not have a "gift" for the person's whose name I pulled. The other children laughed at and ridiculed me for being poor. I remember getting into a playground argument with one of my classmates, who is now one of my Facebook friends, and she proudly shouted out in front of everyone, "My outfit costs more than your whole wardrobe". That statement stuck with me for years. Children, unknowingly, can be very cruel. She had no way of knowing how her words would affect me, and even motivate me.

Fast forward to my high school years, and not much had changed as it related to my financial situation, but what had changed was my mentality. I knew that in order for me to move myself from poverty that I had to be the best and the brightest. I knew that I had to work harder than anyone and everyone else. I knew that I had to be different. I did not want *struggle* to become my middle name.

I was always competing, whether it was spelling bees, the glee club, academic games, or academics in general. The competition helped me to sharpen my saw; it made me better. Competition became an adrenaline rush for me. I found ways to compete at everything to compensate for the lack of material things. I may not have had the latest clothes, K-Swiss sneakers, or book-bags, or sheepskin coat, but I was certainly the brightest in all of my classes. I was even class valedictorian.

I received achievement awards for honor roll and perfect attendance; I was on the student council and was the teacher's pet in just about all of my classes. That's how I learned to even the playing field when I was in middle school and high school.

Poverty pushed me to want more, to do more, and not to accept mediocrity.

When I look back at the neighborhoods that I grew up in, many of the people that I grew up with are no longer alive. Many of them dropped out of school and even more of them continue to live in the same neighborhoods that we grew up in and are continuing the cycle of generational poverty.

Breaking the cycle of generational poverty is difficult, especially when you don't realize that the conditions that you are living in and have lived with are bleak. You learn to simply cope, which is what my mom did. You consider the condition of poverty – your circumstance – to be the norm, because you have never been exposed to anything other than your current condition.

When I became an adult, my past experiences of being reared in an impoverished household were fuel for me to achieve my goals. Against all odds, I completed middle school. Because of my high academic scores, I was accepted to Cass Technical High School and I even went on to college and pursued a degree in accounting.

When I was sixteen, I worked at Elias Brothers Big Boy restaurant on the eastside of Detroit, across the street from Belle Isle. Big Boy was the hang out spot for teenagers and young adults. On weekends, Big Boy closed at four o'clock in the morning, and we would catch the crowd that left Belle Isle at two a.m. when it closed, and they were hungry; or the crowd that just finished cruising the strip on Belle Isle and weren't ready to go home.

On a hot summer Saturday night, I met the man that would become my husband. He came into Big Boy with about eight of his friends, and before he left, he asked for my number. Seven digits and several months later, we were married.

I got married when I was seventeen years old, and not very long after that I had my first child. I was still in my senior year of high school and I actually went to my high school prom with my husband. I had family members tell me that I would never graduate high school and that I would amount to nothing. Those closest to me didn't have faith in me and instead they beat me down with closed-minded rhetoric. Either that was their way of motivating me or they thought that their plight and cycle of generational poverty would become my own, because of the choices that I made to become a young wife and a young mother.

I was married in September 1989. I was scheduled to graduate in June 1990. I gave birth to my daughter in February of 1990. I took three weeks off from school, and I had my husband pick up all of my school work for me so that I wouldn't fall behind. I had to take summer classes in order to be able to walk across the stage and graduate with my senior class; on time and on schedule. I was willing and prepared to do whatever it took to prove all of my naysayers wrong. My goal was to graduate; to graduate *with my class*…and that's what I did!

The State of Michigan would not allow a child seventeen years of age to obtain a marriage license without parental consent. The age of consent was eighteen. Therefore, I had to go to my mother and ask her permission to get married and ask her to sign the necessary documents to allow me to obtain a marriage license. When I came to her, I was four months pregnant, which was partially the reason my mother agreed to allow me to get married in the first place.

My mother, myself, and my future husband, who was 19 at the time, went to the City County Building in downtown Detroit to file our paperwork for a marriage license, and in September of 1989, I was legally married. Five months later, my daughter was born. I had an actual wedding ceremony. My dad's girlfriend; a seamstress, made my gown for me. She was careful to allow a little bit of room for my growing belly. We were wed in the basement of a church that I don't even remember, and surprisingly, my dad gave me away.

As a woman now over forty, when I look back on my mental and emotional state at seventeen years-old, I realize that one of the key motivating factors for getting married was I saw it as a way out of poverty. I didn't plan to have a child at such a young age, but I didn't take the necessary steps to prevent it. One of the strangest things about my now ex-husband was that his parents were still married, and that, too was something I had never seen before. No one that I knew at the time besides my husband was in a home with both of their biological parents.

In my mind, if I was married and had a partner, a team mate, a helpmate and a friend, I would be able to pursue my dreams, the American Dream, and pursue my goals; none of which included being hungry or walking anywhere with holes in my shoes. I think that had it not been for the environment that I grew up in, I would not have made a choice to get married at seventeen, much less have a child.

I truly believe that our circumstances influence who we are, but we are responsible for whom we become. Although I made choices at seventeen that would change the course of my life forever, I was not bound like a mother to an umbilical cord, to the same generational cycle and mentality of poverty that preceded me.

I found myself about to take a trip down poverty lane when I was pregnant with my daughter. My husband was a full-time college student pursuing his undergraduate degree when we got married, and as such, we didn't have medical insurance, therefore, I couldn't get the proper pre-natal medical care that I needed. With the concern of my unborn child in mind, I reverted to what I knew best; ADC. I was seventeen, on welfare and food stamps, just as my mother and grandmother and great-grandmother were before me. This hurt me to the core of my very soul. This was a legacy for which I did not want to become the torch bearer.

Not me; I had to be different. This generational curse had to stop with me. This would not become my life story. Lying back and collecting a check from welfare was degrading in my mind. As an adult, I was embarrassed to go to the store to purchase food with food stamps and WIC coupons or stand in line at Focus Hope, with everyone else that seemed to have given up.

During my middle school years I was excited to get those stamps every month to go shopping, and our trip to the grocery store was a major family event. Now, as an adult, it was humiliating and embarrassing. I knew, however, that this was only temporary. I couldn't or wouldn't live like this.

Being a young mother was no joke. It was not easy, nor was it glamorous. I don't care what you see on TV or how teen pregnancy is glamorized; it is hard. I will be the first to admit the difficulty of raising a child, going to school, working, and being a wife. When I should have been preparing for college, possibly pledging a sorority or simply hanging out with my girlfriends, I was at home changing diapers, teaching my daughter to walk, preparing dinner for my husband, and keeping our house clean. I encountered challenges daily, and those challenges helped me to build character, made me more resilient, made me look adversity in the eye and say "not today".

I did not know the first thing about being a mother, because I was still a child myself. I didn't know the first thing about being a wife, because I had no frame of reference; my parents separated when I was two years old. I had no rites of passage and I made many mistakes as a parent and as a wife. But, there was one thing I did know, and that was academics. That's where I found comfort. That is where and how I was always able to compete.

I made a series of bad choices; some of which I learned from, and some of which I repeated because I didn't get the lesson the first time. Some of those bad choices I'm still paying for today. But, no matter what obstacle I faced, the driving force motivating me was to never realize poverty again.

In 1999, I joined an organization that would have a profound impact on the rest of my life; the *National Association of Black Accountants* (NABA). This organization has done more for me than any other professional organization that I have belonged to or any corporation that I have worked for. NABA gave me the platform to spread my wings and sharpen my saw. I attended my first NABA National Conference in Chicago, and it was by far the most eye-opening experience I have ever had as an African-American woman. For the first time, I was in the presence of 4,000+ black men and women, who all had it going on. That was POWERFUL! It's important to see yourself in successful settings and identify with success. At that NABA conference, I was able to see with my own two eyes successful black men and women, and I thought, *YES, I can do this…I want this…I have to push harder. If they can do it, so can I!*

NABA became my role model for successful black men and women. I wanted to have the same success that I saw. I wanted to be standing in front of a podium speaking to an audience, and I wanted to fly around the world offering financial advice to corporations. I wanted to facilitate a technical session. I wanted to travel the world. I wanted to own my own business. I simply wanted to shine, and make my mother proud, and that's what I did.

NABA allowed me to participate on a committee, lead a committee, become a board member at the local level and regional level, and I even participated on a couple of National Committees. NABA afforded me opportunities that I wasn't given in corporate America, and I was then able to take those transferable skills to my job in corporate America, and I was able to not only shine, but climb the corporate ladder. NABA did that for me.

Today, I reflect on all of the lessons that poverty taught me. I am no longer on welfare. I no longer need to rely on the government to provide basic needs for myself and my family. I broke the cycle of generational poverty in my family. I wanted to show my family; *if I did it, so can you*. Poverty is a state of mind, and breaking that cycle by changing my thinking, was my goal all along.

I am grateful that the governmental assistance was there when I needed it, and I am grateful for the pain and embarrassment that I felt when standing in line to buy food using those food stamps, because that was motivation and fuel for me to push harder. I look at my life now, and for all intents and purposes, I wasn't supposed to make it. According to statistics on generational poverty, on teenage mothers, on growing up in a single-parent household, I'm not supposed to be here; I was destined to continue the cycle.

From worn out shoes, WIC coupons, big blocks of government cheese, meat in a can with a cow on the side of it that read *"beef"* and food stamps, to where I stand today; owning a couple of prosperous businesses, speaking around the world and teaching people how to establish, nurture, and grow business relationships. I went from poverty, worn out shoes, and food stamps, to now teaching diverse audiences about proper dining and business etiquette. I put my recruiter hat on and I coach and teach candidates how to interview, how to properly format a resume, and how to negotiate a salary, benefits, and total compensation package. I teach college students how to make a transition from college to corporate America.

In November of 2010, I published my first book, *"How to Talk to Strangers: A Step-by-Step Guide to Professional Networking"*. In February of 2013, I published my second book, *"365 Days of Motivation: A Guide to Success in Life & Business"*, and I am currently working on my autobiography, *"Behind the Signature Pearls ~ The Tammy Turner Story"*.

I have traveled the world to the most exotic and exciting places: West Africa, West Indies, Hong

Kong, Malaysia, Indonesia, Singapore, Thailand, Japan, and Vietnam. I lived in one of the most impoverished countries in the world; Cambodia, for three years, and I worked for the United Nations as a recruiting consultant. I learned to speak two languages in addition to English, Khmer and Japanese. I was also taught to read and write Hiragana and Katakana. I have also known the luxury of having a live-in housekeeper, a nanny, a driver, and a cook.

I served on the Board of Directors for a variety of successful non-profit organizations and have spoken for major corporations such as Best Buy, Chrysler, PricewaterhouseCoopers, American Society for Training and Development, and National -Management Association. I now own the house that I only dreamed of in the most beautiful neighborhood in the city of Detroit. I also own the fancy car that I once day-dreamed about and I bought it with cash; no financing. I rub elbows with policy makers and politicians that are trying to clean up the neighborhoods that I once grew up in, and I was recently named, by MIX92.3 Radio as one of the "*25 Most Influential Women in Detroit*". I strive to lead by example in all that I say and all that I do, because I know that there are others, just like me, that weren't supposed to make it; that weren't supposed to survive their circumstance.

I met, fell in love with, and married the man of my dreams. I have been a mother to four children and a stepson. Until now, I wasn't comfortable telling my story because I was afraid. When people look at me today, they see a woman that is well groomed, well dressed, and well put-together, but they have no idea of the struggles that I have endured to be in a place today where I no longer live in poverty and I no longer have a poverty mindset. I was nervous about acknowledging those struggles publicly because I was very concerned about judgment and ridicule, and the image that people had of me diminishing. What I realize is that there are so many people that have walked my walk and are still walking the road that I traveled, and they need to have something to strive towards and have hope that it can be done. Oftentimes, our inspireation comes from people that we know have beaten the odds and accomplished great things despite what society has labeled them or what their environment has determined that they should be.

I refused to let my environment define me or let my circumstances handcuff me. I was determined to do and be everything that I desired, and I was determined to let no one and nothing become a deterrent. I changed my thinking and that decision SAVED my life!

I'm not that special. No, I'm not that special at all. I put my pants on one leg at a time, just like you. I was just a little girl with a dream and the "audacity of hope." I was a little girl that believed that if I fought hard, I could have more, do more and live a fruitful and fulfilled life. I even had this silly notion of teaching others to pursue their dreams. How dare I have such high aspirations!? How dare I be a little girl from the hood of Detroit that believed she could?

Success for me isn't having millions of dollars in the bank; although I choose to believe that I'm well on that road. Success for me is leading by example for all of my family to see, that if I could do it, so can they. Success for me is setting goals and achieving them. Success for me is giving back whenever and however I can. Success for me is being able to live, eat, sleep, and breathe my passion, which is public speaking, and getting paid to do something that I love so much that I would do it for free. Success to me is coming home to my dream home, and a loving husband, my children, and the newest addition to our family; Chico, our puppy (keep in mind that I was so poor growing up that having a puppy was out of the question, because it was simply just another mouth to feed). Success to me is traveling the world, living and loving life, meeting new people, and learning from other cultures.

One key lesson that I learned while on this journey was to never make excuses. Excuses are well thought out lies, so I decided to stop making them or using them to justify why I couldn't move forward with my dreams.

When I look back at all that I have accomplished since I was the little twelve-year-old girl with the hole in the bottom of her shoe who couldn't afford to purchase a $2 Secret Santa gift, I stop, pause and smile, and I say a quiet little prayer and give thanks for all of those lessons that brought me to where I am today.

So, give thanks for those character-building moments that you endure, because they strengthen you and equip you with the necessary tools to be successful. Break any generational non-productive and damaging cycles that you are currently involved in, and believe in yourself and all of your abilities. You are equipped with everything you need to be and do, and have everything you desire. You can, and you will win.

If you ever have any moments of doubt or self-pity, I want you to remember the twelve-year-old girl on the swing with the hole in her shoe. She reminds me daily to stay focused and stay the course. She is a living, breathing, walking, talking example that perseverance; a shift in thinking and goal setting are the keys to success. She has the soul of a winner!

Success-isms:

*   Challenge your excuses.

*   Your circumstances may have influenced who you are, but you are responsible for who you become.

* Poverty is a state of mind. It only becomes state of being if you allow it to do so.

5 True Stories of Success

Chapter 3

Potholes to Smooth Roads
By Javay Johnson

Potholes to Smooth Roads

On my road to success, I have had many detours, bumps, pot holes, and turnarounds. I have experienced the highest of highs and have endured the lowest of lows in pursuit of my dreams. I have said some things and done some things that I wish I could take back, but can't. I have made some good decisions in my life and some that I regret. However, one of the greatest decisions that I ever made was the decision to "get help." It takes an immense amount of humility and courage to ask for help sometimes. After all, I am Javay J. Johnson! I have it ALL together! So I thought…

I was *Ms. Positivity*. I founded a company on the principles of positive thinking and the idea that what you expose your mind to can expand. Here I was teaching and talking about being positive to other people, yet I felt like I was drowning in a cesspool of negativity. I would also feel depressed because my vision of myself was not aligned with my reality. I would constantly ask myself, *Who am I? What am I here?* Many days I felt like a fraud.

Who would have ever known that I had a secret buried so deep into my soul that even my closest family and friends had no knowledge of it? I held on to that secret for several years, but now via these words and this paper, I am breaking my silence. I am not breaking my silence for me; I am breaking my silence for other individuals who wish to open themselves up and not live in denial or fear. I am breaking my silence for the world so that it can change in a positive manner. Judgment and stereotypes plague what I will be sharing with you, but the reality is that it does not have to be this way.

In 2007, I was in corporate America doing my very best, but I found it very difficult to get along with my manager. My job became increasingly unbearable to the point that I actually hated going in to work. As the relationship between my manager and I deteriorated, so did my mental health. I would be so stressed out sometimes during and after work. It felt as if there were ants crawling under my skin and an itching sensation would turn into an outbreak of hives. I would go home at night and never have a break from my place of work because I would mentally replay events and ruminate angrily throughout the night. I could not even get a break during sleep because I would dream about the workplace and the workplace "villains." I truly had a hard time coping with my mood that was frequently in an irritated state.

I was also working on my MBA during the particular time that I was having problems with work. Education was supposed to be my escape from my problems, but for some reason, I could never score a grade higher than a C. This was highly disappointing to me because I truly studied hard for exams and completed all of my assignments. I gave higher education my all, but even my best did not seem to be good enough. I felt like a failure in many areas of my life from work, to school, and several of my personal relationships.

I can remember going to my medical doctor and informing him of what I was going through, and he immediately put me on a medical leave from work and gave me a referral to see a psychiatrist. I needed something to cope with my reality, and I thought that time off from work with some rest and relaxation would do the trick. I went ahead and scheduled an appointment with the psychiatrist as directed, thinking that maybe I just needed medication to help me with stress. The psychiatrist prescribed me an antidepressant to help me "get through" my days. While on this antidepressant, I had some weird occurrences that made me go back to the psychiatrist to report my experience. What the psychiatrist said next changed my life forever: *"You are bipolar!"* My heart sank while a chill came over my body. I immediately burst into tears.

My thoughts were scattered at that time. What did this mean? How did this happen? Why me?

In 2008, I was formally diagnosed with Bipolar Disorder II with severe mania and depression. I did not want to believe this news. I didn't want people to treat me differently if I admitted that there was something seriously wrong with me, so I kept it to myself. I was in denial along with being scared and ashamed. I kept this a secret for a long time until now. I am one of the millions of people living in the world with bipolar disorder.

In my culture, mental illness has not been and is not a topic of discussion that people casually speak about. Some people think that mental illnesses are simply categorized as just being *crazy* or *insane*, in which for many mental illnesses that is not the case. There are many functioning individuals in this world who have not been formally diagnosed with a mental illness who are not acknowledged as being insane by the standards of mental health professionals. Many of those aforementioned individuals are suffering silently because they fear the label, the stigma, and the negativity that surround mental illnesses. I believe that there are many individuals in the world who, like me, did not want to accept the diagnosis. I truly had to review my overall quality of life and realize that everything could possibly be better if I actually gave treatment a chance.

Some symptoms of bipolar disorder can include:

Mania

-Euphoria
-Inflated self-esteem
-Poor judgment
-Rapid speech
-Racing thoughts
-Aggressive behavior
-Agitation or irritation
-Unwise financial choices
-Increased drive to perform or achieve goals
-Decreased need for sleep
-Easily distracted

Depression

-Sadness
-Hopelessness
-Suicidal thoughts or behavior
-Anxiety
-Guilt
-Sleep problems
-Low appetite or increased appetite
-Fatigue
-Loss of interest in activities
-Problems concentrating
-Irritability
-Poor performance at work or school

If you believe that the symptoms listed here are indicative of the experiences in your life, then I recommend that you seek advisement from an appropriate medical practitioner who specializes in treating these conditions. Regardless of whether you go the naturopathic route or with traditional medical treatment, the important thing is that you can be seen and evaluated. After all, you are currently living one life right now, so why dismiss your ability to experience a high quality life?

Going through the cycle of depression and mania is what I relate to going through hell. One day I would feel on top of the world like I could conquer anything, and then the next day I would feel like I just wanted to end it all. Life was like a never-ending emotional rollercoaster for me. There were constant highs and lows. I felt as if my life was like a common board game. I would roll the dice and move one step forward, only to roll the dice again to be knocked backwards. This condition affected every aspect of my life. It affected my relationships with family and friends, co-workers, even strangers. My moods would shift like gears of a manual transmission. I was a highly emotional person and a ticking time bomb. I would constantly feel like my emotional cup would "runneth over" and all I needed was one more drop, and that was it! I could not digest criticism, I could not handle disagreements, and I for sure could not handle anything emotional. I was socially incapacitated during this time, in which I spent many hours sleeping because I could not face the world. I was devoid of medical treatment, and I was in denial despite the visible signs that were clear to me at the time.

It was not until 2011, while speaking with one of my family members who was being treated for depression, that I came to the realization that I had to do something to change my life. I could not imagine living the rest of my life in this way. When that particular family member revealed to me that she was going through a similar mental condition and made the decision to have a better quality of life, it hit me. My quality of life stunk and something had to change. Although I have always been surrounded by great friends and family, I would go through instances where I felt like I would never amount to anything positive, and I believed that no one had a value for what I had to offer the world. I struggled with these phases of depression that lasted for weeks, and nothing would help me to snap out of it.

Once I had truly accepted the fact that I had been diagnosed with bipolar disorder and that this was a chemical imbalance in my brain, my life began to change positively. I sought out help for the second time. I was extremely emotionally exhausted from going through an internal turmoil over which I seemed to have no control. I wanted change. I wanted to be healthy. I wanted to be a better person. I wanted to regain the helm of my *spiraling out-of-control* life. I wanted more for myself. I wanted a great future. None of this would happen for me if I did not get the proper help that I needed.

I do not refer to my condition in its common negative connotation. The diagnosis of my condition was a gift to me. Some may disagree with this statement, however, this condition taught me a lot more about myself. I have chosen to harness momentum from this condition rather than to allow myself to live a mediocre life succumbing to stigmas and stereotypes. I believe that I was specifically chosen to endure, learn, and successfully manage this condition. I am bringing about awareness, hope, and inspiration to not only those who have struggled or are struggling with their gift, but for people with loved ones who are living undiagnosed or have not accepted the reality of their diagnosis.

Bipolar disorder for me did have a positive side. I would have these periods of mania that also provided spurts of absolute brilliance and creativity. I have fostered several talents and turned them into business endeavors. I have created and sold abstract art, won poetry slams, designed and sold mustard seed necklaces, coiffed hair, and much more. I consider my creativity to be one of my best qualities.

In researching and understanding bipolar disorder, I have found out that many of the great minds in history have been afflicted with the same condition but went on in life to contribute great things to the world we live in today. As quoted by famed comedian Conan O'Brien, at the 2011 commencement for Dartmouth College, "*It is our failure to become our perceived ideal that ultimately defines us, and makes us unique. It's not easy, but, if you accept your misfortune, and handle it right, your perceived failure can become a catalyst for profound re-invention*". O'Brien's quote truly resonates with me. Failure, setbacks, and obstacles are all integral parts to becoming successful. On your path to success you will experience misfortune, Murphy's Law, and have bad days, but it is truly about how you handle those situations that will ultimately define you and your level of success.

Throughout my dealings with bipolar disorder, on my good days, I was focused on achieving my dreams of becoming an author and a motivational speaker. I can remember at times feeling intense anxiety when asked to speak or facilitate workshops. Many times, I pushed myself to complete the task at hand while inside I was suffering. People's expectations of me were the same no matter if I was going through depression, mania, or if I felt okay. I had to keep up this façade as if everything was ok, and believe you me; that was a tremendous amount of work!

Once I had become stabilized with my treatment plan and therapy, I began to look back on my life and the relationships, jobs, and opportunities that possibly had been affected by my *gift*. There was much light shed upon how I treated and reacted to people such as my fiancé, parents, friends, family, and even strangers. My mood totally affected my attitude and behavior. Simply thinking positive was not working for me. Nowadays I actually have a focal point to which I compare my behavior.

I can recall recently taking an emotional intelligence test that asked specific questions about how I react and handle certain situations. The way that I handle life's situations now are 180 degrees different from how I used to handle things, and that is how I know I have changed for the better. I am a lot calmer now; things that used to make me irate do not bother me as much these days. Before, my anger would be out of control. I could actually feel my anger heighten in levels like an elevator going up passing floors. I used to give the lucky people a verbal disclaimer with not so kind words that stated: "At this particular time, I am not accountable for my behavior!"

Now I feel like I can deal with the world in a new way. In fact, I feel like a totally new person. My fiancé can attest that I am a changed person. Our relationship suffered greatly in the beginning due to the harshness of my words. I commonly spoke out of anger rather than love. It took me to begin treatment with medication and a therapist to see how vicious my words were and how negative I had become. I look back on some of my situations and analyze how I have handled them. Some situations and memories resurface with regret, but all I can do now that I am well is to treat the people around me with love and understanding.

How did I defy the odds and statistics? I never let the many detours, bumps, pot holes, and turn-arounds stop me; not even bipolar disorder. I managed to keep my goals on the forefront during the times that I was feeling well, and after I began treatment, I executed every goal that I set out to accomplish. I wrote and published my first book entitled, *"Success Is Spelled with Two C's The Average Person's 20-Day Guide & Workbook to Becoming Successful"*. I enrolled back into graduate school and currently have a 3.6 grade point average. I also have returned to corporate America to work a job that I love with superiors with whom I get along. I constantly visualized the end result of my goals. Doing visualization exercises kept me motivated and excited because I knew what accomplishing certain goals meant for me. I persevered through it all; the good, the bad, and the ugly. Although at the time of my formal diagnosis I thought that it was the end of the world, I apparently survived it, and I am here today with victory!

On the road to success, you must not give up on determination; with determination you will be able to overcome seemingly impossible odds. Speaking of seemingly impossible odds, whenever I feel like giving in to the face of defeat, I remind myself of the existence of several remarkable people who have overcome seemingly impossible odds:

-**Dan Caro** died three times from a childhood incident that unfortunately burned over 80% of his body, leaving him with no hands or fingers. He is now a phenomenal drummer who received a full scholarship to Loyola University and played in their world-renowned jazz band. He believes that his handicap is not an obstacle.

-**Bobby Martin** was born with Caudal Regression Syndrome, meaning his body ends at his pelvis, no thighs and no legs. He played high school and college football as a defensive tackle and hopes to soon play for a semi-pro team.

-**Bethany Meilani Hamilton** is a professional surfer who survived a shark attack, but lost her entire left arm. Not only did Bethany regroup, practice harder, and return to professional surfing, she pulled 1st place in 2005 and continues to place in high ranks in surfing competitions worldwide.

-**Ben Underwood** (now deceased) had his eyes removed at age two due to retinal cancer. He perfected being able to see with his ears by making clicking noises with his tongue using echolocation; a sonar navigation technique used by bats and by dolphins.

When I think about my struggles and obstacles that I might be facing, including bipolar disorder, I tend to think about the Dan Caros, the Bobby Martins, the Bethany Hamiltons, and the Ben Underwoods of the world. Then I begin to wonder if what I view as an obstacle in my life is truly an obstacle. Even when you think that your situation is unfavorable, there is always someone else who may have other circumstances or challenges that you may find highly difficult to handle if placed in the same position.

A tool that helped me immensely is what I call a self-evaluation inventory. Some may need to do this more than others, but at a minimum, you should conduct a self-evaluation inventory on your life at least twice a year. If you plan to conduct your self-evaluation inventories twice a year, then you will want to select a date, and write down as many accomplishments that you have achieved thus far. Next you will want to write out as many feasible goals that you would like to achieve within the next six months. On the sixth-month anniversary of writing your original list, you will want to first write out a list of what you have accomplished in the previous six months and compare that list to the list you wrote six months ago. In retrospect, you will want to answer some questions, such as, "How many goals from my original list have I accomplished?" "In what ways has my life changed in the previous six months?"

Sometimes, having the ability to see how you have actually progressed is better than just living your life totally unaware of the progress or lack thereof. The data you gather can be used to not only shift your attention to areas of your life in need of repair; it can also be encouragement to aim higher. One of the most remarkable experiences in life is to have a moment when you realize how far you have come in reference to where you began!

Another tool that helped me out in dealing with bipolar disorder was creating a "Mental Health Safety Plan" to use during times when I experienced certain feelings. Below is a snapshot of a safety plan that I constructed for myself:

When I feel anxious in social settings, I can:
- Repeat affirmations to myself
- Ask if the hostess needs some help
- Introduce myself to someone
- Give someone a compliment
- Get a plate of food

When I feel a lack of self-confidence, I can:
- Do visualization techniques
- Repeat affirmations
- Call a friend
- Remember times when I was confident
- Create internal self-talk

When I feel angry or frustrated, I can:
- Meditate
- Take deep breaths
- Remove myself from the situation if possible

- Count to ten
- Visualize a calming image

Having a mental illness does not have to hold you back from achieving your goals and experiencing a higher quality life. There is hope and there is definitely a light at the end of the tunnel. What you may be going through is not the end of the world; it is only the beginning of a fantastic life if you so choose it to be that way. Success does not discriminate; success is available to each and every one of us in abundance despite the circumstance we encounter. True winners embrace adversities and use them to foster better outcomes. We are all faced with challenges, and life may not be easy at times, but those who keep going, keep working, and keep striving for excellence are the ones who will take home the prize.

Having courage and commitment will take you further than you could ever imagine. Never let anything hold you back from achieving your goals. It is a true fact that pressure makes diamonds, so be encouraged to shine bright and enjoy the experience of having the soul of a winner!

Success-isms:

* Seek out help from an appropriate medical professional if you feel that you may be suffering from a mental illness.

* Remember that having a mental illness does not have to define your existence.

* Failures, setbacks, potholes, and turnarounds are all a part of the road to success; it is how you handle those failures, setbacks, potholes, and turnarounds that determine how much you will succeed.

Chapter 4

From Bus Stop to Won't Stop
By Hugh Lee Johnson

From Bus Stop to Won't Stop

The view from my apartment balcony in Santiago de los Caballeros, Dominican Republic, is what dreams are made of. An incredibly blue sky and a mountain range that stretches as far as the eyes can see. I couldn't help but think that this is what success is all about – peace of mind, beautiful surroundings, and the time to enjoy it all with your family. One thing's for sure; this international lifestyle that I am living is a long way from where I was just a few years ago.

No matter what your definition of success may be, achieving your idea of success will require knowledge, commitment, and action. Success will not float down from the heavens and land in your lap. I'm a true believer that dreams do come true if you use the proper tools and take the necessary actions to progress forward on your journey.

Within the next few pages, you will learn some helpful tools, tips and strategies to take you from where you are today to where you want to go in life and in business. Locked within every page of this book are the keys to your success. As you experience this book, it is important for you to understand that at this very moment, you possess everything within you that is necessary to achieve any goal that you could ever dream of.

My life's journey is now your personal lesson book. The mission is to help you activate the personal powers that you were born with so that you can use those powers to win in life. Winning in life, love, and relationships is the true sign of wealth and freedom. You, your family, your community, and the world have something spectacular to gain from your success.

As the famous Notre Dame football coach, Knute Rockne said, "All the world loves a winner and has no time for a loser". Winning and losing in life are a choice. It is my goal here, now and into the future, to play an active role in your success as a natural born winner. There's nothing that can stop you because you have the power to win.

Now, prepare your mind, body, and soul for a powerful change. Turn the page and let's make it happen together…

On a cold October night in 2004, there was only one question on my mind: "Can I make it till the morning sleeping in this bus shelter?"

It was pretty damn cold that night in Oak Park, Michigan, and I just wasn't sure. It wasn't like I had any past experience with being homeless. But here I was, unable to pay my rent after a garnishment of my part-time paycheck.

All that was certain at that moment was that I felt so embarrassed. You see, I always considered myself a pretty smart person. At the age of 12, I tripled the size of my paper route from 45 customers to 145 customers in less than six months. I graduated from Detroit's premier high school, Cass Tech, and began attending at Lawrence Tech, School of Architecture, at age 17. I possessed a positive outlook on life and was an entrepreneur at heart. But despite all of that, there I sat in the cold, nearly in tears, wondering if I would live or die if I fell asleep in that bus shelter. On that cold night, I made myself a promise – no matter what it took, I would learn the secrets of success, put those secrets into action, and then share the lessons with others.

Something told me to call my mother. I had hesitated earlier because I did not want my shortcomings to become a burden on my parents. As my mother and I spoke, she could hear the pain in my voice. I told her where I was, and she invited me to return home for a warm and comfortable sleep. Ashamed but relieved, I agreed.

More determined than ever, I began a new mission to make a positive shift in my life. I wanted to prove to my parents that they had made a good decision in inviting me back into their home. After a short period of time, my hustle and hard work started to show results. This was the start of something good.

Eight months after moving back home with my parents, I was able to move into a rental home with my brother, Oliver, on Detroit's Westside. Thanks to my father, a retired member of UAW Local 600, a local steel factory called me concerning a temporary position. After a series of test, I was hired as a temporary employee with the possibility of becoming permanent after 89 days. From the first day I started working at the steel factory in the shipping department, I wasted no time in showing my foreman that I was a dependable hard worker who was hungry for the opportunity that I had just received. Word of my work ethic spread fast throughout the department.

My reputation as the *go-to* man for overtime grew with each passing day. Despite my reputation as a good worker, I was laid off just short of 89 days in August of 2005. By that time I had already planted the seeds of being a dependable worker in the hearts and minds of all of the foremen. Without a doubt, it would be my work ethic that would save the day. Thinking that I would be called back to work within 30 days, I didn't worry.

The call to return to work as a permanent employee wouldn't come until early January 2006. To my surprise, I was met by my foreman and co-workers alike with hugs and handshakes. What had taken place to get me to this point?

In just over a year, with hard work, a positive attitude and determination, I went from near homelessness to a permanent job making a high five figure income; not bad! I knew that this opportunity was just a stepping stone though. To my core, I am an entrepreneur, and no high-paying job could ever cure me of that. In the realm of jobs, I had a pretty decent job. Some factory workers in Detroit can make between $70,000 to $120,000 per year.

The money that I made from 56 hours of work only took two hours to spend. I couldn't help but feel that something was wrong with that equation. Don't get me wrong; I wasn't splurging on fancy dinners, alligator shoes and champagne bubble baths. I did have bills, grown children who needed my help, and grandchildren. Paychecks can disintegrate upon impact in certain instances, and mine were one of those instances. Something had to give, and I knew it.

I was grateful for a new beginning, but I knew something had to change. My solution at the time was to work more hours. That is when I entered into a distinguished league of co-workers who I like to call "The Heavy Hitters." Heavy Hitters are the employees who consistently work 80-112 hours per week. A master crane operator named

Forrest would be my coach and mentor. Little did I know at the time that Forrest would be instrumental in helping me professionally and personally for years to come.

After six months of working ungodly hours, I was finally taking a little break. I was on my way to Santiago de los Caballeros, Dominican Republic for a long weekend. Two months earlier, I had met a beautiful Dominican woman named Sandra, through an online dating site. Her enthusiastic email and text messages won my heart. Before I took things any further with her, I wanted to confirm that she was as sweet in person as she was in her messages.

My plane landed at Cibao International Airport, mid-afternoon on June 24, 2006. I remember the day well because I declared it a holiday; "Honey's Day." Speaking very little Spanish at the time didn't stop me; I was ready for a new adventure and a new wife. After my first marriage fell apart 13 years earlier, I had dated several women looking for that "one".

I'm still amazed at how many women complain about not being able to find a good man but who act a fool when one appears. Being committed to achieving the goal of becoming the good man to a good woman, I began making a mental list of all of the qualities that I like in a woman. I didn't focus on looks; only on qualities. This mental list of qualities became my vision of a good woman.

As fate would have it, 3,000 miles from Detroit, at the smallest international airport that I have ever seen, I met that woman. And guess what? She didn't speak a word of English, and I couldn't speak Spanish. But that was all right because from the moment that I saw her beautiful smiling face peeking from behind her sister and best friend at the airport, I knew that she would be my wife. In my heart, I knew that someday that I would cross paths with that special woman. What I didn't know is the when or the where. In the end, none of that mattered.

Two months after meeting the woman of my dreams in person, I was prepared to put a ring on it. While preparing for my return to the Dominican Republic, my friend and co-worker Mike requested an hour of my time one afternoon so that he could talk to me about a business opportunity. I smelled a multi-level marketing sales pitch coming on, but I couldn't just blatantly say no to a friend without giving him a chance.

My plan was to wait until after Mike's presentation, then to gently turn down his offer to join his MLM organization. I'd had dreams of being a successful entrepreneur for a long time, but I wasn't crazy about the MLM business model. Over the past 30+ years, I had tried several different businesses from being an airbrush artist to insurance and investment sales. You may have heard the entrepreneurial saying, "Follow your passion". Well my introduction to entrepreneurship at the tender age of 12 had very little to do with passion. It had more to do with frustration.

In the early seventies, a couple of months before my twelfth birthday, I would walk into my father's workshop every Saturday and ask, "Daddy, my friends and I want to go to the movies today. Can I have five dollars?" My dad would reply, "Why, should I just give you five dollars? When I was your age, nobody gave me anything." My father's $5 sermon would go on for about 20-30 minutes, and then he would reach into his pant pocket and hand me a $5 bill. Have you ever seen a 12-year-old boy's hair turn gray? Gee-whiz! You would have thought that I asked for my Dad's last $100 and the keys to his favorite car. The experience was nerve wrecking. But I would always walk away with the money and have a fun-filled day with my friends. Five dollars went a long way in the early seventies.

After five or six of these $5 sermons, I couldn't take it anymore. One morning I showed up at the neighborhood newspaper station to inquire about how old I had to be to start delivering newspapers. The station manager informed me that I had to be 12. With excitement in my voice and a twinkle in my eye, I told the station manager with the enthusiasm of a big game lottery winner that I would be 12 in one week.

The following week I returned to the paper station to lock down my new paper route. As luck would have, there was an available route right in my neighborhood. When I started, the route had 45 customers. After learning the paper route game, I quickly took over two other connecting routes, which more than tripled my customer base to 150 customers. Things were never the same after that. Sometimes not getting what you want is really a blessing in disguise. At one of our weekly coffee outings, I thanked my father for the $5 sermon experience.

So here I was with this mysterious opportunity that Mike wanted to offer me. When I asked him what type of opportunity it was, he simply avoided answering me. He just said, "Don't worry about it. You're going to watch a DVD." As I prepared myself mentally for Mike's presentation, I thought about what I had learned over the years from trial and error in trying to build a successful business. With each failure and every small success, I developed a mental list of the qualities that I thought an ideal business had. And despite the fact that I was in search for a good business opportunity, in my mind, I was ready to let my friend Mike down easy after his DVD presentation.

Soon after arriving at my home, Mike didn't speak much. He just popped a DVD into the player for me to watch. The video was of a talk given by a young business man named Mr. Bostic. In the video presentation, Mr. Bostic covered the 10 key ingredients of an ideal business. You're not going to believe this, but those ingredients matched my mental list. Go figure!

Was this a weird sign or something? Needless to say, I couldn't pass up the opportunity. After two face-to-face interviews, I became a member of the CNG Mentorship Program and an Amway Representative. Two weeks later, I was on my way back to the Dominican Republic to propose to the woman of my dreams.

Not sure how to propose in Spanish, I knew that I needed help. I had recently met a young perfume merchant from the Dominican Republic at the local mall, so I paid him a visit. With a pen, he wrote the magic words that I would use in my marriage proposal on a small piece of paper. He then read the word to me, making sure to pronounce each word slowly. I repeated each word back to him. It was clear that I lacked Spanish-speaking skills, but after a couple of practice runs, I thanked him for his help and he wished me luck.

A week later, I was on a plane to Santiago de los Caballeros, with a diamond ring and that little piece of paper with my marriage proposal written in Spanish. I rehearsed that proposal all of the way from Detroit to Santiago. On August 28, I asked Sandra to marry me – in Spanish – and of course she accepted. We were married two days after her birthday on December 2, 2006. If you ever have doubts that you can have what you want out of life, brush those doubts aside and remember that dreams do come true. I know because mine did.

Newly married and on a mission to achieve an international lifestyle, I dove headlong into learning the secrets to a living a financially free life. My goal was to become a master of time and money. The mentorship program was a means to that end.

My life changed when Mr. Bostic suggested that I read T. Harv Eker's book, *"Secrets of the Millionaire Mind"*. Within the book was an invitation to attend a free three day *Millionaire Mind Intensive*. The invitation sounded very Interesting, so after a little research, I found that there was a *Millionaire Mind Intensive* coming to Chicago, just a five-hour drive from Detroit. The Intensive was no longer free though. A $99 materials fee was required, but that did not matter; it was a small price to pay, and I was in it to win it.

It was the spring of 2007, and I arrived in Chicago by bus the evening before the three-day intensive seminar. I was filled with excitement, but excitement quickly turned into sadness when I crossed the threshold of my hotel room. The last few times that I stayed in a hotel, Sandra was always with me. This time she wasn't. She was still waiting for me in the Dominican Republic. Pushing through the pain of not having my new wife with me, I prepared myself for what would unfold over the next three days. There were 1,500 people in attendance from all over the world, all on a mission to transform their lives and the lives of their family.

During one exercise on the second day of the Intensive, I volunteered to go on stage with a half dozen other attendees. When it came my time to speak, I briefly shared my bus stop story and declared that I would become a millionaire within 18 months; a bold statement that didn't come true, but there were greater things in store for me.

A couple was so touched by my story that they offered to take me to lunch during our midday break. The couple was a very sharp looking husband and wife business team. We spoke about our reasons for attending the seminar and then the husband made a confession to me. He said, "Hugh, I know that we look rich on the outside, but we're cash poor." It's amazing how we can judge people by their outer appearances without knowing anything about them. Throughout my journey, I have seen rich people who looked poor and poor people who looked rich, but what is it that makes people rich or poor? Is it the dollars in their bank account? Is it the clothes that they wear or perhaps the car that they drive? I have realized from personal experience that what makes a person truly rich are their thoughts and their actions. So although the sharp couple I met in Chicago was cash poor, their thoughts and actions – the very fact that they invested their time and money to be present at the *intensive* – made them rich.

There have been times in my life when I didn't have much food to eat and could barely pay rent, but I have never considered myself poor. On the flip side, I have had money where living expenses and international travel expenses were not an issue, but that didn't make me rich. Wealth and poverty are born in the mind and manifested into the physical through your actions. You are the Master of your thoughts, so choose – yes, you do have a choice – to be a good Master. The alternative is to live your life like a drunken master with negative thinking and excuse making.

While my fellow participants in the *mentorship program* were reading books on financial freedom and personal growth by well-known authors, I was traveling across the country to see those same authors speak. My physical experience of attending live seminars further enhanced my reading experience and provided me with a connection that the people in the *mentorship program* lacked. My life was transformed because of what I experienced through countless books, training programs, and the live seminars that I attended.

The gist of what I have shared with you so far is that learning can lift you up above being a victim of life's challenges, and transform you into a student of life's lesson. You may not have the means to travel across the country to attend live seminars, but don't let that stop you. Use books, audio CD programs, and free online webinars to get started. Commit yourself to investing a portion of your income to learning. What should you learn? Well, that depends on your passions, and your frustrations.

For learning the skills that will get you closer to your goals, take time and sit down with a pad and pen, and write down your passions and frustrations and use them as your map to win in life.

Love has a way of blinding you sometimes. I know because I've been blinded on more than one occasion. After a year and a half of marriage, my wife still had not received her Visa to join me in the United States. Every two to three months, I would jump on a plane and travel from Detroit to Santiago to spend a week or two with her. At the time, we were renting a huge 4-bedroom apartment just a fifteen minute drive from the international airport. Marble tiled floors, polished wood trimmed closets, more square footage than two people really needed, all for $250 American per month. Incredible! Add another $40 for utilities and our household expenses, excluding food, was still under $300 per month. Compare that to over $1,000 in monthly household expenses in the U.S. and a culture structure on work to pay bills. Although I had a "good job" in the U.S., life in America did not represent freedom and the enjoyment of time and family. On the other hand, the Dominican Republic represented time with my wife, freedom to really savor good food, beautiful weather, and a different perspective on life.

Life in the Dominican Republic is not what most people think. Yes, there are struggles with money for many, but there are three things that Dominicans lack that Americans have plenty of: Debt, compounded interest of debt, and heavy taxation.

Many Dominicans own their cars, homes, and businesses. Life in many cases is not easy, but the people hustle and make it happen. With each trip to the Dominican Republic, I learned new lessons of what time, financial freedom, and family really meant. Each time that I had to return to the U.S. without my wife was a painful, tear-filled experience. Something had to give.

It was June 2008 and I was on my way back to Santiago to spend a month with my wife. A last minute *leave of absence* form was submitted over the weekend, and I was on a plane to Santiago that Monday. Not much of a plan, not much savings, but still excited with being with my wife.

After three weeks of living my new lifestyle in Santiago, I received an alarming text message from Mike, my friend from the steel plant. His message informed me that the plant was about to fire me and that I needed to get back to work within two days. Without a passport, that wasn't going to happen. The United States had changed travel laws and a passport was needed to fly from foreign countries into the U.S., which meant I had to travel using trains, planes, and automobiles, and stop off in Puerto Rico before I could fly back to Detroit.

By the time I made it back to Detroit, I was fired because I didn't give my foreman advanced notice that I wanted to take a leave of absence. He refused to approve my request – 5 Day No Call, No Show. Damn, damn, damn! What was I thinking? Wall Street crashed, and so did I. The only difference was that Wall Street would be bailed out by the American taxpayers; I wouldn't.

It would be October of 2008 before the Union could get me rehired at the steel factory. By that time, my lights and gas had been turned off at the house that I was renting. Another Detroit winter was quickly approaching. Even though I was back to work, I still wasn't making enough to have my utilities re-established. It's amazing how much colder the inside of a house can be when you don't have any heat. Sometimes the air can be too cold to breathe.

To sleep at night, I would use an ugly sweater that an ex-girlfriend gave me years earlier, as leggings to keep me warm. I would simply turn the sweater upside down and pull the sweater's sleeves over my feet and legs. I used fleece blankets that I received while flying Delta Air to wrap around my body and make a cocoon. Those blankets were excellent for holding in my body heat while I slept.

To this day, I have never shared with my wife the hardships that I experienced while we were apart. I didn't want to burden her mind and emotions with my struggles. My life in America was on fire, and the only escape was my positive thoughts backed by focused action. I understood without any doubt that everything I was experiencing would make me a better leader in the future.

All struggles pass. Every hurdle that you will face in life will be cleared. The Real Secret is that you were born with the mind of a Creator, the heart of a Giver, and the Soul of a Winner. If anyone tells you anything different, remember one thing, "The devil is a liar."

In Mid-August of 2012, I punched out for the last time at the steel plant and tossed my work boots in the trash. For years, it had been my goal to live an international lifestyle with my wife. Now that dream was about to come true. It had been a year and a half since Sandra first arrived in the United States. We now had a baby daughter, and we were both homesick for the Dominican Republic. Yeah, it's strange, I was born and raised in the United States, but I still got homesick for my wife's country when we were away for too long.

We had secured a brand new three bedroom apartment not far from my in-laws. We were the first family to move into the new complex and the noise-free environment was enjoyable. The view from the apartment's patio balcony was spectacular; a mountain range as far as the eye could see, draped by the bluest sky. With excitement in my heart for our new life together, and my wife and my baby in my arms, I could not help but to feel blessed.

I am blessed because of the people who were sent into my life to help with my growth and transformation. I am blessed because I learned the right lessons at the perfect time. But most of all, I am blessed because I didn't quit – I have the soul of a winner!

Success-isms:

*   ABL: Always-Be-Learning

*   Wherever positive thought and action are present, failure is impossible.

*   Success begins where the fear of failure ends. Failure is an important part of learning and growing as a person. Winners understand that in order to become good at anything, they will most likely stink at it first.

5 True Stories of Success

Chapter 5

A Leap of Faith: Finding the Courage to Follow Your Dreams
By Chris Lee

5 True Stories of Success

A Leap of Faith: Finding the Courage to Follow Your Dreams

It was 3:00 p.m. I had returned from my break, and my password did not work. I was unable to unlock my workstation. I stood up to walk over to my manager's desk, but he met me at the end of my row. We made eye contact with each other, and I wasn't quite sure what to make of the semi-stern expression on his face.

"Follow me please, Mr. Lee," he said. He then walked me into the conference room and said that he'd be right back. I nervously paced in the darkened conference room. The décor was outdated; its chic had expired twenty years ago.

There was a whiteboard with dried out erasers and generic paintings from the 1980's. I walked over to the window and looked out into the forgotten part of downtown Detroit. One day soon a permanent MGM casino would be built in this spot. Right now however, there was a row of abandoned townhouses, empty buildings, and a few half-empty parking lots.

The window was filthy. The grime always made the outside look a little darker than it actually was. I had been in this room at least once a week over the last 11 years, but this was the most tense I had ever felt in the big conference room.

My silent stream of consciousness was now broken by my supervisor, Windell. He was a tall man with dreadlocks. He was always a very professional person with a composed self-assured spirit. "This shouldn't take too long Chris," he said in his trademark calm demeanor.

I had been re-assigned to his department a few months earlier in January of 2010. It was now the last day of May of 2010. I had been miserable the entire time, although I did my best to make it enjoyable. Today though, this would all come to an end.

Windell invited me to sit down. I sat across the table from him, and a few moments later, Windell's manager joined us. "Ok Chris," the big boss said, "we're going to do your exit interview." I wasn't sure what to say. I wasn't sure how to feel either. Although there were horror stories about the big boss floating around the office, my limited interaction with him had been positive. We began the exit interview. It was very impersonal; a series of yes and no answers to questions that didn't really matter.

When we were done, they asked for my badge and my *SecurID* token. I slid them across the table, and my supervisor gave me a packet of papers with his personal cell phone and email address scrawled across the front. "If you ever need anything, don't hesitate to call," he said, looking me squarely in the eye. I appreciated the offer but felt like I hadn't gotten to know him well enough over the last four months to actually use the number. I was guarded with my new supervisors even though I didn't need to be.

All three of us stood up, and we shook hands with each other. Jon, the big boss, said, "Chris, we appreciate your years of service and wish you the best of luck in your new endeavors." I felt a sinking feeling as I smiled and thanked him politely. This was supposed to be one of the most auspicious days of my life; my escape from corporate America! Instead, I felt I was walking the plank.

I stepped outside of the room, and there were several people who were also either retiring or accepting a buy-out package as had I. They all had boxes and bags. Some people were tearful with mixed emotions.

I didn't have anything to take with me except for those papers I had just been handed by my boss and a couple of other things. I had been displaced and reassigned so many times that I didn't have anything of personal value in my work area.

We all boarded the elevator, rode to the main floor, and were then escorted out of the building. I would never be able to get into that building again; I was now a visitor; a very unceremonious ending to my corporate career. I had always imagined a fancy cake from my workmates and a nice going away party at a downtown bar. When another workmate left the year before, we stood and applauded as he took his final walk. We were so proud of him. He was leaving to start his own trucking company. He had a definite plan, and he began executing it right away.

That close-knit department had been disbanded and scattered throughout the company, so I would receive none of that. I received a card signed by people that I didn't know from my new department, and a tiny gold pendant with an embossed *AT&T* logo.

I had always dreamt of working for myself in the capacity of helping people; educating them and liberating their minds from negative ways of thinking. Around 1996, I began entertaining the idea without a real action plan; just a dream that felt good. That's all it was…just a dream. Until an interesting run of events took place, beginning in 2007.

In 2007, I was involved in a serious automobile accident. At the time it seemed like the worst thing that ever happened to me. I missed eight months of work; it turned my life on its ear. I even sustained a mild traumatic brain injury (TBI). You can read about the journey to healing and recovery in my book, *"From Frustration to Fulfillment"*.

Having a TBI totally changed my life. I was now a different person, and re-acclimating to everyday life was a tough task. There was a silver lining, however! After the accident, I began to realize that my life actually had a purpose. I nearly lost my life, I was still here for a reason, and I began to explore that reason.

I went back to work at *AT&T* after a nine month recovery time, and it was a real struggle. Prior to my accident, my job was cushy and comfortable. By this time, I had begun to talk about leaving, but it was really more like a disgruntled teenager threatening to run away "one day." The biggest factor driving my desire to venture out on my own was the fact that I was resisting the changes at work.

Over the next year or so, all of that would change. One of the things that helped me to heal was *energy medicine*; the treatment of the subtle body (the energy field surrounding the body). I began clearing negative thought patterns that I had been carrying for years. As a result, I began having a really clear understanding of what I really wanted out of life. Personally, I wanted more meaningful relationships, and professionally, I wanted to have a positive impact on the lives of millions of people.

I began learning, studying, and practicing everything I could about energy medicine, emotions and the power of the subconscious mind. Then around December of 2009, something beautifully synchronous happened. As I completed several certifycations, and my confidence as a practitioner grew, a date popped into my head: May 31, 2010. I meditated upon that date and researched it and couldn't come up with anything. I couldn't figure out what the significance of the date was until March of 2010.

I had experienced a setback with my health and was off work on disability. My phone rang and it was Jenna, one of the supervisors from *AT&T*.

"Hello, may I speak with Chris Lee?"

"This is Chris."

"Hi Chris, this is Jenna from work. I know you're probably not interested, but per the contract (CWA collective bargaining agreement) I have to inform you that *AT&T* is offering a buyout in lieu of possible layoff."

"Wow, okay," I said. "Send me the paperwork; I actually might be interested." I then asked, "When would my last day be?" To which she replied, "May 31, 2010."

My mouth literally hit the floor. That was, of course, the recurring thought that I had been having. It's what I had been calling my message from the Universe. What would I do for a living? Should I get another job? What's the meaning of all of this? Obviously, it's bigger than me!

Had that date not been stuck in my head, I may not have even entertained the thought of leaving the "security" of my job. However, when Jenna spoke the date that had been stuck in my head since December, I realized that I had a greater purpose, and I was now being called into action.

To even be in a position to hear the voice of a higher power, I had to heal my life. My accident did just that. While I did suffer serious physical injuries and a brain injury, there were deep unresolved emotional issues that came to the forefront during the healing process. Because of all these unresolved emotions, from about the age of 15, I battled various addictions. After the accident, I was put into a position where I had to deal with my emotions, and it accelerated my healing. I felt like a new man, like I had a heavy weight lifted off of my shoulders. I wanted as many people as possible to experience emotional freedom. Now I was being presented with the opportunity to do so!

The last three years, despite ups and downs and setbacks, have been some of the most rewarding times of my life. I have helped dozens of people to discover their purpose, to heal from the past, and to let love into their hearts.

Many of us are closed off to receiving love on a subconscious level, without realizing it. Initially I was one of those people. One of the most interesting things that I've come to realize is this: The work itself, the work of a healer, is not limited to a specific profession. When I first started out, I was doing nutritional counseling and energy work with my clients. That work has morphed into a few different things; workshops, consulting, creating informational products and so forth, but the core "work" is still the same. My goal is still the same also, regardless of the entrepreneurial hat that I'm wearing at the time.

If you look hard enough, you will find healers in your life, too. It could be a hairdresser, a workmate, a certain musician, a minister, a holistic practitioner, and so on. In this context, when I speak of a healer, I'm simply referring to someone who helps you to transcend suffering. A healer is someone that makes you feel better when you're around them.

The Universe has a way of connecting the healers with those that need healing. Although there are hundreds of healing modalities, millions of therapists, practitioners, and psychologists, these are a few simple things that help people to heal:
-Music
-Laughter
-Pets
-Hugs/Human Touch
-Prayer/Meditation
-A Judgment-Free Listener
-Unconditional Love

If a person needs professional help, that's fine. Just know that there are ways to bring joy into your life and the healing process will begin. In actuality, your body was designed to heal itself; physically, mentally, and emotionally. When we get "stuck" in a certain state of being emotionally, that's what actually causes imbalance, which leads to *dis-ease*.

Under the proper conditions, your body will heal itself. The truth is, each of us has the capacity to help others to heal. Every time we pray for someone, or hug someone, or silently send love to someone, we take on the role of healer.

As mentioned, my life after taking the corporate leap has been very rewarding. Entrepreneurship has had its ups and downs, but all in all, I have very few regrets about following my calling. The life of an entrepreneur can be a very busy life. In many ways, I traded in one boss for many bosses. Keeping your clientele happy is one of the most important duties of a business owner.

There are times and situations that are "gut-checks". There have been times when I wasn't sure how I was going to make rent or keep the lights on, but I always found a way. Braving tough situations builds character and confidence. The biggest gift that I've gained from taking the leap is a new mindset: I believe that I can do anything that I put my mind to.

"All creation is one." – Ralph Waldo Emerson

American poet and pioneer thought-leader Ralph Waldo Emerson suggested that all humans and all nature are in fact connected. That means that anything that one of us has accomplished, any of us can accomplish. With that truth in mind, what is it that you want to accomplish? What is your purpose? What is your ambition? Whatever it is, you can do it! It all starts in the mind: Success, failure, happiness, sadness, jealousy, contentment, and joy. The thoughts we think and the words we use have a profound effect on our mental and ultimately our physical wellbeing.

Our subconscious mind is a very powerful thing, BUT it cannot decipher between what is real and what is not. That is why, if you have a nightmare, you will experience elevated heart rate and rapid breathing. Or, if you are worried about a future event, you will tend to experience stress about a situation that hasn't happened yet. The reason is your subconscious mind doesn't know that it's not really happening. Our thoughts cause our bodies to have a physical response to those thoughts.

This phenomenon, however, works both ways. When we visualize success, our subconscious mind doesn't know whether it's happening for real or not. We do it all the time for negative situations; flip the script and start creating or manifesting your desired outcome. It really works!

You are perfect just the way you are. When you were a small child, you knew this, but along the way, you changed who you were to please others; your parents, your teachers, your friends, etc. Thus you became misaligned with the real you.

Fortunately, after reading this, you're aware of it and can begin thinking about what your priorities, beliefs, and goals really are. What is it that you truly want to attract into your life based on a pure and clear vision of self-awareness?

When I speak of success, it's up to you to define what success means to you personally. Consistently coping with addiction, overcoming a handicap, mending relationships, and similar things are all very worthy goals and are deserving of the use of the word success. When you start to pursue your success, you will begin to hear a voice in your head that will say to you, *"You're not good enough, you can't do it"*. You may blame someone else who may have actually said those words to you before, in jest or in seriousness (incidentally, the words are just as damaging either way). However, the true origin of the thought is you.

You may begin to wonder or even ask, *"Am I good enough?"*, but trust that you are good enough, and that you can achieve your definition of success.

Regardless of what you've been through, whomever you recognize as your Higher Power wants the very best for you, without anything in return. So with that in mind, ask yourself this: What are you drawing from for motivation? Your own negative thoughts, or the power and infinite love of the Divine?

Success-isms:

* ***Visualize success*** - Exercise your success muscle by envisioning success. There may be other skill sets to learn to achieve your goal, but continue to visualize the end result that you desire.

* ***Give yourself proof that you are good enough*** - What have you been successful at in the past? What goals have you reached so far? All of these are proof that you can set a goal and reach a goal, even tiny ones. A baby-step is still a step forward.

* ***Now is the perfect time to start on your goal*** - You don't have to get it right, just get started. Don't allow what you believe are obstacles to slow you down. Where there is a will, there is a way. There is no time like the present.

About The Authors

Versandra Kennebrew

Tammy L. Turner

Javay Johnson

Hugh Lee Johnson

Chris Lee

- Versandra Kennebrew -

Health is mind, body, and spirit working in symphony, and **Versandra Kennebrew** is an optimal health conductor. She has educated hundreds of massage therapists and other holistic health professionals. Through her empowerment tools, retreats and presentations, she supports health seekers all around the globe on their journey towards optimal health, balance, and fulfillment.

An innovator, Kennebrew has reinvented herself and her business several times and is currently on a mission to support thousands of holistic health enthusiasts. As a certified myomassologist, energy field enhancement specialist, aromatherapist, international public speaker, homeless advocate, philanthropist, social media strategist, and self-improvement teacher, Versandra Kennebrew has a plethora of tools in her holistic health tool-box.

In 2003 after a number of major life challenges, Kennebrew lost everything and became homeless. This experience connected her more deeply to her mission, to touch the world. Her memoir, "Thank God for the Shelter," chronicles the process of getting back up after a knock-out and gaining enough strength and power to not only stand but to run a marathon. Her second book, "The Art of Reinventing You," takes readers on a journey into their own creative mind, the ultimate resource for inventing. These self-help books are the foundation of her speaker repertoire.

Ask anyone who knows Kennebrew and they will likely say, "She does a lot to help people." Her philanthropic efforts have supported hundreds of Detroit area homeless families. Her passion and her love for humanity drives all that she does. Versandra Kennebrew believes that every human has special gifts and talents that when nurtured and fed, have the power to shift darkness into light.

To request Versandra Kennebrew as a speaker for your college, university, church or conference, please visit:

www.thesoulofawinner.com

- Tammy L. Turner -

Tammy L. Turner is a Recruiter, Author, Public Speaker, and Trainer. Tammy is the owner of Kapstone Training Services, LLC and Kapstone Publishing. Tammy is also an Engineering Recruiter with d. Diversified Services.

After serving for over six years in the field of public accounting and having worked at major firms such as Arthur Andersen and Deloitte & Touche, Tammy realized that her true passion was in the field of Human Resources. As such, Tammy worked as a recruiter for Robert Half Finance & Accounting and a senior recruiter at Quicken Loans/Rock Financial. In 2004, Tammy was able to travel overseas to Cambodia where she worked as a recruiting consultant for UNICEF. Tammy returned to the United States in 2007 and established Kapstone Training Services, and in 2010, she established her own publishing company Kapstone Publishing.

Tammy's "Elements of Success" program has helped shape the careers of students and business professionals throughout the U.S. and abroad. In this program, she offers training on executive presence, business etiquette and image, dining etiquette, leadership training, and skills to successfully master the art of networking. Her debut book, *How to Talk to Strangers: A Step-by-Step Guide to Professional Networking*, is a vital tool for any business professional looking to go to the next level. Your mother may have told you not to talk to strangers, but Tammy teaches you how to talk to them. Tammy published her second book, *365 Days of Motivation: A Guide to Success in Life & Business*, in December 2012, and it is a must have for anyone and everyone looking for encouragement or inspiration in their daily business or personal relationships. Tammy was also recently named one of the "25 Most Influential Women in Detroit".

Tammy enjoys watching football, loves to ski, and is an avid golfer. She enjoys spending time with her husband Lance, her children, and their dog, Chico.

To contact Tammy for speaking engagements, please visit:

www.thesoulofawinner.com

- Javay Johnson -

Javay Johnson is a proud native Detroiter, philanthropist, and graduate of Dr. Martin Luther King Jr. Senior High School - Detroit, and (I.U.P.U.I.) Indiana University-Purdue University - Indianapolis. For years, her passion has been in helping others to succeed in life. Currently the C.E.O. of Javay Johnson LLC, Javay has formally been in business since 2004.

Beyond being an author and motivational speaker, Javay obtained a graduate certificate in Project Management from Walsh College in Michigan, and has several years of experience working in the career services industry for higher education corporations.

With the release of her first book, *Success Is Spelled with Two C's - The Average Person's 20-Day Guide and Workbook to Becoming Successful*, Javay inspired, enhanced, and enriched the lives of many people. What separates Javay from others is her delivery of a fresh perspective, her ability to connect and relate to the struggle, and the fact that she speaks genuinely from real life experiences.

Javay has reached thousands through her motivational testimony of struggle to success and has is affectionately referred to as "The Life Remodel Specialist." She focuses on teaching individuals the foundations of making better life decisions that elicits better outcomes. A self-made mogul in her own right of a growing enterprise, Javay has experienced several obstacles. One obstacle that she has overcome beyond the diagnosis of bi-polar disorder is having to transition from a homeless shelter. She serves as a role model and inspiration to her peers, family, and friends.

Javay won the *Alternatives for Girls* "Role Model of the Year" Award and is in the 2011 5th edition of *Who's Who In Black Detroit*. Javay's experiences have spanned from being an entrepreneur, instructor, to a director on a college's executive management team. Her techniques and expertise have also been noted through her contribution to 'Job Search Expert' articles, published in *The Detroit News* Newspaper (11/13/2008 & 01/01/2009).

Javay Johnson is a rising star that everyone should keep their eyes on! She resides in the Metro-Detroit area with her fiancé Michael and their Bichon Frise, Cartier. Javay is available to facilitate "*Success Is Spelled with Two C's*" seminars and is available for speaking engagements. To order additional copies of *The Soul of a Winner* and to learn more about Javay Johnson, please visit:

www.thesoulofawinner.com

- Hugh Lee Johnson -

Hugh Lee Johnson is a serial entrepreneur, business growth consultant, speaker, and the founder of *Digital Publishing Insider*. He is dedicated to helping entrepreneurs and business owners get more traffic, more leads, and more sales.

With over 30 years of experience in personal growth and business sales and marketing, Hugh is an indispensable resource who will coach, train, and inspire your company or organization to success. Hugh's global mission is clear; to engage, entertain, and educate entrepreneurs and business owners to new levels of achievement through live events and web-based training.

Hugh lives both in the United States and the Dominican Republic with his wife Sandra and their daughter, Erika. He's the father of four, and the grandfather of three. Hugh enjoys learning, teaching, and international travel. To learn more about Hugh Johnson, please visit:

www.thesoulofawinner.com

- Chris Lee -

Chris Lee has a passion for helping people to identify and successfully manage the self-imposed limitations that hold them back from pursuing and achieving their biggest and boldest dreams, goals, and ambitions. Using warmth and humor to help people "open the doors of change", Chris is a dynamic speaker and energetic workshop facilitator. Chris has put his unique skill set to use helping numerous people throughout the U. S. and Canada. He combines the Law of Attraction and the philosophy of energy medicine to offer a very unique and powerful experience for those that attend his workshops and coaching sessions.

Chris is also the author of *From Frustration to Fulfillment*, a book written to help anyone that has ever faced a seemingly hopeless situation. Chris uses writing to help others re-discover and reconnect with their true selves because a person armed with "knowledge of self" can accomplish anything.

Chris is a *Specs Howard School of Media Arts* graduate and he currently holds certifications as a 365-Degree Manifestation Consultant, Certified Law of Attraction Facilitator, Certified Natural Health Professional, and Body Talk™ Access technician. To contact Chris Lee please visit:
www.thesoulofawinner.com

About Impact Writers

Impact Writers LLC is a publishing company which produces products which positively impact the lives of people around the world. Our mission is to positively impact the world around us by producing quality empowerment products that inspire and motivate.

We sincerely hope you've enjoyed this book. For more information about our other products, please contact us through the Soul of a Winner website:

www.TheSoulOfAWinner.com

CPSIA information can be obtained
at www.ICGtesting.com
Printed in the USA
FSHW021909180421